Arctic Ocean

A

SWEDEN

EUROPE

S   I   A

A

AFRICA

Pacific

Ocean

Indian

Ocean

AUSTRALIA

ANTARCTICA

# Sweden

## Charles Phillips

Susan C. Brantly and Eric Clark, Consultants

**NATIONAL GEOGRAPHIC**
WASHINGTON, D.C.

# Contents

# Foreword

The third-largest country in Western Europe, but with a population smaller than Belgium, Sweden is more sparsely populated than Brazil, and is among the countries of the world located farthest from the Equator. Sweden has large forests covering over half the country, long coastlines, and numerous islands (a recent official count reached more than 220,000) and lakes, all of which are accessible to the public thanks to Sweden's unique tradition of "allemansrätt," or the right of public access. The Swedish countryside is probably more accessible than that of any other country.

Sweden is also widely known for its leading role in the development of the modern social-democratic welfare state. During a few decades in the 20th century, Sweden was transformed from a poor farming society, from which many people emigrated to seek fortunes elsewhere, to one of the world's most prosperous and sophisticated industrial nations, with a high quality of life and almost no poverty. The transformation was based on Sweden's wealth of natural resources and technological ingenuity, but it also involved powerful union organization, egalitarian ideals, and a far-reaching redistribution of resources to ensure general access to basic human needs such as health care, education, and housing.

The so-called Swedish model means that all people have access to publicly financed health care, child care at preschools, schools, higher education, elder care, pensions, social services, and economic security systems such as paid sick leave and unemployment insurance. Parents are allowed paid leave of absence to care for infants, and all employees have a minimum of five weeks paid vacation per year. Sweden has remained a market economy, but its wealth has been shared among the

whole population to a greater extent than perhaps any other country. Often called the most generous general social welfare system in the world, the Swedish model has been emulated in other countries.

Nearly half of the elected members of the Swedish parliament, the Riksdag, are women, and Sweden's ideals of equality and solidarity extend beyond its borders. In recent years it has received more immigrants and political refugees in proportion to its population than any other European country. Sweden has become a multicultural society, increasingly enmeshed in global society. Sweden engages actively in international peace efforts through the United Nations, offers aid to poor and developing countries, and creates initiatives for sustainable development and dialogue on global environmental issues.

▲ Houseboats and pleasure craft are moored alongside 18th-century palaces next to Strandvagen, one of Stockholm's most historic streets.

Eric Clark
Lund University,
Sweden

# Sunshine
## and
# Snow

**M**ANY BEAUTIFUL GROUPS of islands lie around Sweden's long coastline. The islands shelter calm waters where Swedish people love to sail, fish, and swim. Inland are many powerful rivers and thousands of lakes. Most people in Sweden live in cities, but they keep vacation cottages along the coast and in the countryside.

Sweden lies in the far north of Europe. The country is extremely long—from north to south it is 977 miles (1,572 km), about the distance from Detroit, Michigan, to Dallas, Texas. The north is level with Iceland, and is part of the frozen Arctic. Here the winter is hard and very long. It does not end until May. But in Skåne, in the far south, the climate is far milder. Spring arrives in March, and people go outdoors to enjoy colorful flowers.

◀ A hiker takes a rest by a mountain stream in Sarek National Park in the north of Sweden. The stream is swollen with water from snow melting on the park's peaks.

# WHAT'S THE WEATHER LIKE?

The weather in the north of Sweden is very different from the weather in the south. In the far north, the winter is very long and cold. The temperature is often around -4° F (-20° C) and can fall as low as -40° F (-40° C). But in the south, the weather is milder in winter and quite warm in summer. Winter temperatures are often around 30° F (-1° C), and in summer they reach over 77° F (25° C). This is because an ocean current linked to the Gulf Stream brings warm waters from the Gulf of Mexico to the region.

The map opposite shows the physical features of Sweden. Labels on this map and on similar maps throughout this book identify most of the places pictured in each chapter.

## Fast Facts

**OFFICIAL NAME:** Kingdom of Sweden
**FORM OF GOVERNMENT:** Constitutional monarchy
**CAPITAL:** Stockholm
**POPULATION:** 9,045,389
**OFFICIAL LANGUAGE:** Swedish
**MONETARY UNIT:** Swedish krona
**AREA:** 173,732 square miles (449,964 square kilometers)
**BORDERING NATIONS:** Finland and Norway
**HIGHEST POINT:** Kebnekaise 6,926 feet (2,111 meters)
**LOWEST POINT:** Lake Hammarsjön −7.91 feet (-2.41 meters)
**MAJOR MOUNTAIN RANGES:** Skanderna
**MAJOR LAKES:** Vänern and Vättern
**MAJOR ISLANDS:** Öland and Gotland in the Baltic Sea
**MAJOR RIVER:** Klar-Göta

## Average Temperature & Rainfall

Average High/Low Temperatures; Yearly Rainfall
**MALMÖ:** 53° F (11° C) / 41° F (5° C); 24 in (60 cm)
**GÖTEBORG:** 53° F (11° C) / 41° F (5° C); 22 in (56 cm)
**STOCKHOLM:** 50° F (10° C) / 39° F (4° C); 22 in (56 cm)
**ÖSTERSUND:** 42° F (6° C) / 34° F (1° C); 13 in (33 cm)
**PITEÅ:** 45° F (7° C) / -6° F (-21° C); 20 in (51 cm)
**KIRUNA:** 50° F (10° C) / 7° F (-14° C); 19 in (48 cm)

MAP KEY
Continental
☐ Cool summer
Mild
☐ Marine west coast
Polar
■ Tundra

Norwegian Sea

Gulf of Bothnia

North Sea

Baltic Sea

0   mi   200
0   km   200

SWEDEN
*Atlantic Ocean*
*Eurasia*
*Africa*

*Norwegian Sea*

Kebnekaise
(Highest point in Sweden)
6,926 ft
2,111 m +   ~Lapland~
Jukkasjärvi
Kiruna
*Viribaure*
SNOW
SCULPTURE,
page 15   NORTHERN LIGHTS,
page 14
+ *Sarektjåkkå*
2,089 ft
6854 m
HIKER TAKES A REST,
pages 2, 6–7
AND
SANDBANKS AND
RIVER CHANNELS,
page 12
SKIER UNDER
MIDNIGHT SUN,
page 13
ARCTIC CIRCLE

*Norrland*

Luleå
Piteå
Skellefteå

Umeå

S W E D E N

Östersund
*Indalsälven*
Örnsköldsvik

*Helagsfjället* + *Storsjön*
5,892 ft
1,796 m

Sundsvall

FINLAND

*Gulf of
Bothnia*

Bollnäs
Sälen
*Siljan*
Mora

*Åland*

NORWAY

LAKESIDE CABINS,
page 14

Gävle
Sandviken

*Svealand*

Uppsala
Västerås
*Mälaren*
Örebro
Stockholm
*Sandhamn*
Södertälje

ESTONIA

*Göta
Canal*
Smögen
*Hornbargasjön*
*Vänern*
*Hjälmaren*
Norrköping
Linköping
*Fårö*
ROCKS ON BEACH,
page 11

SEA TRAFFIC,
page 10
Borås
Göteborg
Jönköping
*Vättern*

*Gotland*

LATVIA

DENMARK
*Kattegat*
*Bolmen*
Halmstad
Kalmar
*Öland*

*Skåne*
Helsingborg
Lake Hammarsjön
(Lowest point in Sweden)
-8 ft
-2.41 m

*Baltic Sea*

MAP KEY
⊛ National capital
● Selected city
+ Elevation

0   miles   100
0   km   100

Copenhagen ⊛ Malmö
*Öresund Straits*
BRIDGE,
page 10

LITHUANIA

RUSSIA

*Physical Map*

*Skagerrak*

*Klarälven*

*Ångermanälven*
*Umeälven*
*Vindelälven*
*Skellefteälven*
*Piteälven*
*Luleälven*
*Kalixälvern*
*Torneälven*
*Muonioälven*

~Kölen Mountains
(Skanderna)~

# Scandinavian Neighbors

Sweden and two of its neighbors, Norway and Denmark, form a geographical region known as Scandinavia. To the northwest, Sweden's border with Norway runs through the Scandinavian mountain range. Many peaks are over 6,500 feet (2,000 m) high. Farther south,

▲ The Öresund Bridge, here being built, joins Sweden to Pepper Islet, an artificial island. The new island got its name from its natural neighbor—Salt Islet.

western Sweden faces three stretches of water that separate it from Denmark to the southwest. These are the Skagerrak, the Kattegat, and the Öresund straits.

Today a high-tech bridge and tunnel cross the Öresund strait. They connect the city of Malmö in southwestern Sweden to Copenhagen, the capital of

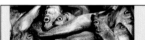

## THROUGH THE CAT'S THROAT

Southern Sweden is surrounded by narrow ocean channels. The Kattegat, or "Cat's Throat," lies between western Sweden and northern Denmark. It is a vital link from the Baltic Sea to the North Sea and the Atlantic Ocean. The Kattegat is a very busy shipping route, particularly with vessels heading to and from Göteborg, which is Sweden's largest port. Tourists flock to the area in the summer. In Sweden they visit the scenic Kullaberg nature reserve on the shore of the Kattegat. The Kattegat is 137 miles (220 km) long, but only 37 to 88 miles (60 to 142 km) wide.

◄ A mixture of pleasure boats and cargo vessels makes the Kattegat a crowded waterway.

Denmark. The bridge carries a two-lane freeway in each direction and a two-track railroad. It runs from Malmö to an artificial island where cars and trains continue into an underwater tunnel that connects to Copenhagen. All together the bridge-tunnel is 10 miles (16 km) long.

Sweden has a border with a third neighbor, Finland, in the northeast and faces the Gulf of Bothnia and the Baltic Sea farther south. In the winter, the Gulf of Bothnia freezes over. Two large islands in the Baltic Sea, Gotland and Öland, are part of Sweden. They are famous for their meadows of wild orchids. Some kinds of orchid live nowhere else in northern Europe.

## *Made by Glaciers*

Sweden's landscape was carved by ice. Great glaciers or sheets of ice moved across Scandinavia about 10,000 years ago. They rounded the tops of mountains, cut steep-sided valleys, and made Sweden's 100,000 lakes.

Almost one sixth of Sweden lies north of the Arctic Circle. The landscape is nearly bare. Trees cannot grow because the summer is short and the winter is so cold. Beneath the top layer of soil,

▼ Rocks on the island of Fårö, near Gotland, have been eroded into columns by the wind and the sea. The island was a backdrop for the movies of the famous Swedish movie director Ingmar Bergman, who lived there.

11

much of the ground is frozen all year round. Shrubs, grasses, mosses, and lichens are all that live here. The land is called tundra. The name means "treeless upland" in the language of the Sámi, the people that traditionally live there.

Farther south, the vegetation is rich. There are miles of forest, snow-capped mountains and glaciers, and wetlands. In the south lie rolling plains and farmland, and sandy beaches face the Baltic Sea. Most of Sweden's industry is in southern Sweden. The main cities—Malmö, Göteborg, and the capital, Stockholm—are all in this part of the country.

# MIDNIGHT SUNSHINE

**S**weden's Arctic north is known as "the land of the midnight sun." In summer the sun never sets. The area is bathed in sunlight 24 hours a day. But the summer lasts only three months, from May to July. In winter the sun does not rise above the horizon. It is dark or half-light for months on end. This is known as "Arctic twilight." Farther south, the rest of the country also benefits from long days in high summer. Even in Stockholm, in southeastern Sweden, the night sky does not fade beyond twilight in midsummer. The nights are just four hours long. In the middle of winter, however, the days in Stockholm are very short and the nights seem to go on forever.

▼ A skier slides down a slope—in the middle of the night.

## *Baltic Islands*

Just outside Stockholm harbor, an archipelago, or group of islands (in this case 24,000 islands), begins and stretches 50 miles (80 km) into the Baltic. Some of the islands have no buildings or inhabitants. Others can be reached by ferry. Some people live on the islands and others keep traditional wooden vacation cottages. These islands often have hotels and youth hostels. The islands are especially popular with sailors, bird-watchers, and nature lovers. The Royal Swedish Yacht Club is on the island of Sandhamn. Each summer people arrive there from many countries to take part in the famous Round Gotland yacht race.

# INLAND WATER

Like other landscapes made by glaciers, Sweden has many lakes. The largest is Lake Vänern in the southwest. Lake Vänern is about 90 miles (145 km) long and more than 40 miles (65 km) wide. On three sides Vänern is surrounded by rocky shores, but to the south there is farmland. It is very beautiful. In the middle of the lake, a group of islands form the Djurö National Park. Lake Vänern is a great center for fishing—35 different species of fish live in its waters. The lake drains to the west through the Göta River into the Kattegatt. To the east it is connected to the Baltic Sea by the Göta Canal. Using the canal, ships can pass right across Sweden between the Baltic and North seas.

▲ Swedish lakes are all public property. All Swedes have the right to swim and sail in any lake.

## Light Shows

The Arctic north is a good place to see one of nature's most spectacular displays: the aurora borealis, or "northern lights." These displays of green or red light in the night sky are caused by collisions between tiny particles very high up in the Earth's atmosphere. The

▼ The northern lights fill the January sky in this view from the Icehotel at Jukkasjärvi in northern Sweden.

light shows usually appear in fall and spring—but you have to stay up very late to see them. Often they don't start until 11:00 PM or even later.

## Snow and Ice

All of Sweden is snowy in winter. In the south the snow only lasts a month or two, but in the north it covers the ground from mid-October to mid-April. In Kiruna, the northernmost city in Sweden, the snow can be up to 7 feet (2 m) deep.

Every January Kiruna has a "snow festival." Teams compete to carve sculptures from huge blocks of ice. Near Kiruna, at Jukkasjärvi, a hotel is built from ice each winter. The Icehotel attracts visitors from all over the world. They wrap up in thick furs and sleep on beds made from solid ice. The hotel is built every November but it melts every April.

▲ This snow sculpture, called *The Slaves*, won the Kiruna snow festival in 2004. It was created by two Polish artists.

Toward the end of winter, 15,000 skiers take part in the Vasaloppet ski race. The race covers 55 miles (90 km) across the country from Sälen to Mora in central Sweden. It was first held in 1922 and is the oldest—and longest—ski race in the world.

# Loose Moose

**O**N FOREST ROADS IN SWEDEN, a special sign warns drivers to beware of elks that sometimes appear suddenly from the trees. Although these antlered deer are called elks, they are far bigger than American elks. They are actually the European version of the American moose.

Sweden's elks are part of a unique range of wildlife and plants that live in the country's varied landscapes, from the frozen tundra of the far north to the fertile lowlands of the south. Northern Sweden contains some of Europe's last areas of wilderness. Visitors from all around the world hike into the wild hoping to glimpse arctic foxes, brown bears, golden eagles, and wolverines or wolves, as well the European moose and the reindeer herded by the local Sámi people.

◀ The antlers of this European bull moose, or elk, will come off when they are full grown. Moose grow new antlers each spring and shed them in winter.

# NATIONAL PARKS

Sweden was the first country in Europe to protect its natural landscapes when it created nine national parks in 1909. Today, 28 national parks, together with many smaller nature reserves and wildlife sanctuaries, cover about 10 percent of Swedish territory.

The parks range from mountainous areas in the north to far smaller forest parks in the south. The rugged Padjelanta, in the northwest, includes Virihaure, which is often called Sweden's most beautiful lake. The Sámi people are allowed to let their reindeer herds wander through the park. The park's snow-fed streams are clean enough for people to drink from.

In the northern Baltic region, the Haparanda Archipelago National Park is a group of sandy islands. Farther south, parks such as Fulufjället and Tresticklan protect areas of ancient forest and the animals that live there. In the far south, Stenshuvud National Park contains heaths, beaches, and broad-leaved woodlands. The map opposite shows the vegetation zones—or what grows where—in Sweden.

▶ **Wolves were nearly extinct in Sweden before a group of animals arrived from neighboring Finland. The numbers are still low, so the animals are not really a threat to farmers' livestock.**

## Species at Risk

Sweden's mountains, wetlands, and forests provide habitats for many endangered animals and birds. The country is also a center for efforts to save species at risk of extinction, such as the arctic fox. The fox is critically endangered: There are only 150 left in all Europe. The sea eagle is an example of how a conservation program can help a species. Once nearly extinct, there are now 350 adult pairs and 900 young. Strict laws protect other rare animals in Sweden, such as the brown bear, musk ox, and otter. Species at risk include:

> Arctic fox
> Bechstein's bat
> Eurasian otter
> European mink
> Golden eagle
> Harbor porpoise

> Pond bat
> Western barbastelle (bat)
> White whale
> Wolf
> Wolverine

## MAP KEY

**Primary vegetation zones/ecosystems**

Boreal forest (Taiga)

Temperate broadleaf and mixed forest

Tundra

**Protected lands**

National park

CLOUDBERRY, page 20

*Muonioälven*

Vadvetjåkka N.P.

Abisko N.P.

Kiruna

Stora Sjöfallet N.P.

WOLVES, page 18

Padjelanta N.P.

Sarek N.P.

ARCTIC FOX POUNCES, page 21

Muddus N.P.

*Kalixälven*

*Luleälven*

ARCTIC CIRCLE

*Torneälven*

Pieljekaise N.P.

*Piteälven*

Haparanda Archipelago N.P.

*Norwegian Sea*

BROWN BEAR, page 20

*Skellefteälven*

Kölen Mountains (Skanderna)

**Norrland**

*Vindelälven*

*Umeälven*

*Ångermanälven*

*Indalsälven*

Storsjön

Skuleskogen N.P.

Sanfjällets N.P.

ICE FISHER'S HUT, page 23

**FINLAND**

*Gulf of Bothnia*

Fulufjället N.P.

Siljan

CALLING BIRD, page 22

*Klarälven*

PURPLE FLOWERS, page 22

**NORWAY**

**Svealand**

Uppsala

Västerås

*Mälaren*

Vänern

⊛ Stockholm

Tresticklan N.P.

Göta Canal

Djurö N.P.

*Hjälmaren*

**ESTONIA**

Norrköping

*Vättern*

Linköping

DAMAGED TREE, page 23

*Skagerruk*

Göteborg

Jönköping

*Gotland*

**Götaland**

*Kattegat*

Öland

**LATVIA**

*Baltic Sea*

**DENMARK**

Kullaberg Nature Preserve

Malmö

Stenshuvud N.P.

**LITHUANIA**

*Öresund Straits*

**RUSSIA**

o miles 100

o km 100

# Vegetation & Ecosystems Map

## Animals in the Wild

Brown bears live in forests and mountains in the northern half of Sweden. They are very shy, and people hardly ever see them. The bears eat ants, bees, berries, and roots. They also hunt salmon, voles, and larger animals—even deer. In late fall bears build a den from twigs and moss, and then hibernate for the winter.

▲ A brown bear stands up in the snow to try to catch the scent of any prey. The animals have poor eyesight.

▼ Cloudberry is a favorite wild fruit for animals and humans—it makes great ice cream.

The northern forests are also home to wolverines. Despite their name, wolverines are not a kind of wolf. They are related to badgers and otters. They look like large brown badgers with bushy tails. Wolverines are protected, but people kill them because they attack reindeer. Only about 450 live in the wild.

Wolves were extinct in Sweden until 1977, when ten wolves entered the country from Finland or Russia. Since then they have been breeding, and today around 150 wolves live in Sweden's forests.

Other rare animals found in northern Sweden are the arctic fox and the lynx. Arctic foxes are brown in summer but change to pure white in winter for better camouflage in the snow. The lynx is the biggest wild cat in Europe—it is known as "the tiger of the north."

## Right to Roam

Swedes love the countryside. Everyone has the right to hike, ski, cycle, or ride a horse anywhere, as long as they follow certain rules. They must not camp close to a private house, walk on cultivated fields, or walk in an area that has been fenced in. This is called *allemansrätt* ("everyman's right"). People are also free to swim or sail on lakes and rivers, and to pick wild berries, mushrooms, acorns, and beechnuts.

## Food in the Wild

Swedish people love wild foods. In spring they rush out with thick gloves to pick the first nettles to make into soup. In summer they pick all sorts of wild berries. In fall they collect different berries and mushrooms.

Beginners go to classes to learn which wild berries and mushrooms are safe to eat. On Monday mornings, workers in cities such as Stockholm and Malmö often have fingers stained with berry juice after a weekend trip to the countryside.

## Flowers and Blossoms

In the long, dark winters Swedes look forward to the return of spring. In March they visit meadows in the south as they fill with spring flowers. In cities you might see people standing on the street, enjoying the

▲ A sequence of images shows an arctic fox diving into a seal's nest hunting for pups. Its fur has turned white for the winter.

sunshine. People watch blossoms come out on different trees. Many Swedes say that the time between the blooming of the bird cherry and the lilac blossoms (usually in May) is the most beautiful time of the year.

▲ Purple geraniums grow wild in Swedish woodlands.

▼ The capercaillie is one of the largest birds in Sweden.

## Bird Paradise

Bird-watching has been popular in Sweden since the 1700s, when the Swede Carolus Linnaeus named most of the bird species of Europe. Today, people come to see rare species such as the great gray owl. In forests

they look for the three-toed woodpecker and the great black woodpecker. In wetlands they might see the whimbrel, ruff, and curlew.

Each spring, visitors to Lake Hornborga in Västergötland watch thousands of cranes as they migrate to northern Sweden, where they nest. The northern mountains are

## THE CATALOG OF LIFE

Carl Von Linné, better known by his Latin name Carolus Linnaeus, was a Swedish botanist in the 1700s. A botanist is someone who studies plants. Linnaeus loved flowers beginning at a young age. At the age of eight he was called "the little botanist." Later, he invented a method for naming plants and animals that is still used today. In Linnaeus's scheme, every living thing has a Latin name in two parts. The first part gives its group (genus). The second part gives its kind (species). Humans are called *Homo sapiens.* They are of the genus *Homo* and the species *sapiens.* The French philosopher Jean-Jacques Rousseau wrote of Linnaeus, "I know no greater man on Earth."

# BURNING RAIN

**M**any of Sweden's lakes, rivers, and forests have been damaged by acid rain caused by pollution from industrial nations to the west and south, mainly the United Kingdom and Germany. Power plants there release sulfur, which makes the water vapor in the atmosphere more acidic. When the vapor falls as rain, the acids carried in the water damage trees and contaminate lakes and rivers. One sixth of Sweden's 85,000 lakes and one third of its rivers have been damaged by acid rain. Swedish scientists try to limit the effects of the acid by adding lime to the water. Because rain runs into the ground, acid also harms the soil below the surface. Factories in the United Kingdom and Germany now have to limit the sulfur they release into the atmosphere in smoke.

▲ Acid rain damages leaves, making it difficult for a tree to get nutrients, and poisons the water in the ground, leading to the death of the tree.

also home to the golden eagle. This huge bird—its wingspan is almost 6 feet (2 m)—is called the kungsörn or "king's eagle" in Sweden.

## A Land for Fishers

With its long coastline and many lakes and rivers, Sweden is a great place for fishing. Fishers can even

▲ A fisher sets up a hut over the hole he has made in the ice of a frozen lake.

catch salmon in the Strömmen Channel in Stockholm. The water there was once badly polluted but now has been cleaned up.

Inland, Lake Bolmen in Småland covers 70 square miles (180 sq km) and contains 365 islands—a different island for every day of the year.

# *War* and *Peace*

**K**ALMAR SLOTT IS ONE OF SWEDEN'S most important castles. First built in the 1100s, it was known as "the key to Sweden"—if an army captured Kalmar, it could conquer the country. In the 1500s, Swedish kings rebuilt Kalmar Slott. It became as much a luxury palace as a stronghold. But Kalmar and other castles are reminders of Sweden's warlike past. Kalmar gave its name to Sweden's 14th-century union with Denmark and Norway.

Today, Sweden is neutral. If war breaks out, Sweden does not back either side. Swedes have often been important peacemakers. In the 1950s diplomat Dag Hammarskjöld set up the United Nations peacekeeping force. In the 1970s and 1980s, former prime minister Olof Palme was an international peace campaigner.

◀ **Kalmar Slott was originally built as a defensive tower to guard Kalmar's medieval harbor, but was rebuilt in a Renaissance style in the 1500s.**

# ANCIENT CIVILIZATIONS

**P**eople first came to Sweden about 10,000 years ago at the end of the last ice age. They moved around to hunt reindeer and gather fruit and nuts. As the ice melted, people moved farther north, traveling by boat across lakes and along rivers. Archaeologists have found remains of their flint tools, bows and arrows, and spears for hunting fish.

▲ An ancient grave is marked in the shape of a ship on Gotland island. Swedish chieftains were sometimes buried in real ships as a sign of their power and wealth.

Beginning in about 4000 B.C., people in southern Sweden settled down and began farming. They grew crops and kept cattle. They built burial mounds for their dead, and made carvings and paintings on rock. In about 1500 B.C. the southern Swedes began to trade by boat across the Baltic Sea and along the Danube River into mainland Europe. On their voyages the traders learned how to make bronze. All this time in northern Sweden, people were still living as hunters and gatherers.

In the first centuries A.D. the Swedes traded with the Roman Empire. The Roman author Tacitus referred to Swedes as "Suiones" in *Germania*, written in A.D. 98. He said they were strong men, with fleets of boats and powerful weapons. This is the oldest written reference to the Swedes.

## Time line

This chart shows some of the major periods of Swedish history.

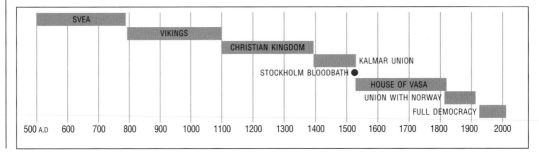

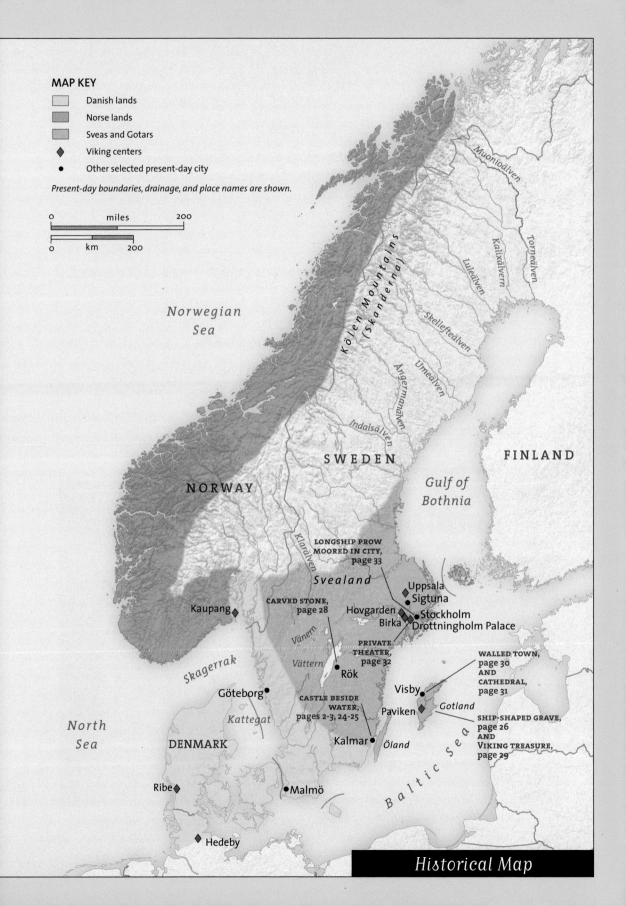

## MAP KEY

- ░ Danish lands
- ▓ Norse lands
- ▒ Sveas and Gotars
- ◆ Viking centers
- ● Other selected present-day city

*Present-day boundaries, drainage, and place names are shown.*

miles 0 — 200
km 0 — 200

*Norwegian Sea*

Muonioälven

Kölen Mountains (Skanderna)

Kalixälven

Torneälven

Luleälven

Skellefteälven

Umeälven

Ångermanälven

Indalsälven

**SWEDEN**

**FINLAND**

*Gulf of Bothnia*

**NORWAY**

Klarälven

LONGSHIP PROW
MOORED IN CITY,
page 33

*Svealand*

Kaupang ◆

CARVED STONE,
page 28

◆ Uppsala
Sigtuna

Hovgarden ●
Birka

● Stockholm

Drottningholm Palace

*Vänern*

*Vättern*

PRIVATE
THEATER,
page 32

WALLED TOWN,
page 30
AND
CATHEDRAL,
page 31

● Rök

Visby ●

*Gotland*

Göteborg ●

CASTLE BESIDE
WATER,
pages 2-3, 24-25

Paviken ◆

SHIP-SHAPED GRAVE,
page 26
AND
VIKING TREASURE,
page 29

*Kattegat*

*North Sea*

**DENMARK**

Kalmar ●

*Öland*

*Baltic Sea*

Ribe ◆

● Malmö

◆ Hedeby

*Skagerrak*

## Land of the Svea

In about A.D. 500, the warlike Svea tribe became powerful in southeastern Sweden. When their kings died, the Svea buried them at Uppsala, north of modern Stockholm. Uppsala was home to the royal palace and a temple where the Svea worshipped the gods Odin, Freyr, and Thor.

The Svea gave Sweden its name. The Swedes call their land Sverige, which means "land of the Svea."

## The Viking Age

Beginning in the late 700s, the Svea and other tribes from Sweden, Norway, and Denmark launched raids along the coasts of northern Europe. They were called Vikings, from the word for "pirates" in the raiders' Old Norse language. In their longships, the Vikings raided

## WHAT DOES IT ALL MEAN?

The world's longest inscription carved in runes is at Rök in Östergötland, Sweden. Runes are letters cut in stone by Germanic and Scandinavian tribes from the 200s to the 1600s. Nobody today can fully understand the carvings. The runes at Rök were probably carved in the 800s on a stone erected by a man named Varin in memory of his dead son. The carving mentions Theodoric the Great, who was king of a Germanic people called the Ostrogoths in about 500. Another part mentions the god Thor. The Rök runestone is the oldest known piece of Swedish literature.

▲ A visitor takes a photograph of the stone at Rök.

# TRADERS IN THE EAST

Swedish Vikings voyaged across the Baltic Sea and up the Volga and Dnieper rivers into what is now Russia and beyond. If they had to, they carried their longships overland from one river to the next. Eventually they reached Constantinople (modern Istanbul) in Turkey, which they called Miklagard ("the big city"). The city was the capital of the Byzantine Empire, and some Vikings became bodyguards for the Byzantine emperor. Swedish Vikings also reached the Caspian Sea and gained access to lands farther east. They grew rich on trade and founded the city of Kiev in what is now Ukraine in A.D. 900. They brought silver, gold, and beautiful cloth back to Sweden.

▲ These artifacts dug up from a wrecked Viking ship include Arab coins that may have reached Sweden through Constantinople.

as far as Spain and Italy. Later, they were the first Europeans to cross the Atlantic Ocean and land in North America. Many Vikings were pirates who simply stole from people they raided. Others settled in the places they reached and began farming. Still others were traders. Swedish Vikings traveled across the Baltic Sea and down rivers into Europe. They grew rich trading slaves, honey, furs, and amber.

▼ Viking sailors battle a storm in their longboat. Longboats usually sailed close to the coast, because crossing the open sea was risky.

## Christian Sweden

The first Christian missionaries reached Sweden in the 800s and 900s. In 1008 Olof Skötkonung, a chief from

Västergötland, was baptized into the church. Olof proclaimed himself king of Sweden. He and his successors fought against pagans until, in the 1100s, Sweden became Christian.

## Trade and Union

In the 1300s German traders became powerful in Sweden. They were from the Hanseatic League, a group of trading guilds based in northern Germany. The Hanseatic traders had bases at Stockholm and at Visby on the island of Gotland. Other trading towns also grew. Swedish nobles became rich and powerful.

In 1389 Swedish nobles revolted against King Albrecht. They were backed by Queen Margaret of Norway, who also controlled Denmark. Albrecht was defeated, and Margaret's grandnephew Erik was

▲ A fly trapped in amber. Made from tree resin, amber was used to create jewelry and was widely traded.

▼ Visby, on Gotland, grew wealthy in the Middle Ages because of Hanseatic merchants.

crowned king of Sweden, Norway, and Denmark at Kalmar in 1397.

The three members of the Kalmar Union quarreled. In 1471 the Swedes defeated King Christian I of Denmark. In 1520 the Danish king Christian II invaded Sweden. He invited Swedish nobles to a banquet—where he had 82 of them beheaded in what is known as the "Stockholm Bloodbath."

## Gustav Vasa

The noble Gustav Eriksson Vasa escaped the massacre. He raised an army and drove Christian II from Sweden. The Kalmar Union was over. On June 6, 1523, Gustav was elected king of Sweden. Swedes still celebrate the date as National Day.

Gustav strengthened the monarchy and changed the army. Armies had usually been called together to fight wars, then sent home. Gustav's army stayed together whether or not there was a war.

When Christianity in Europe split into Catholicism and Protestantism, Gustav adopted a form of Protestantism called Lutheranism. The state took control of the possessions and land of the Catholic church.

Until now, Sweden's kings had been elected from the nobility. In 1544, parliament changed the

▼ Visby Cathedral was originally built in the late 12th century, paid for with taxes raised from German ships using the port. When Sweden became a Protestant state, the church became Lutheran.

rules. The crown would now pass to the king's descendants. Gustav's family, the house of Vasa, ruled until 1818. In the 1600s kings such as Gustav II Adolf made Sweden one of the most powerful countries in Europe, conquering land around the Baltic. In 1709, however, Sweden was defeated by Russia. Ten years later, much of the king's power was transferred to the Riksdag, or parliament.

▲ Gustav II Adolf was one of the most talented military leaders in European history. He was so religious that he often led prayer meetings for his men on the battlefield.

## Age of Enlightenment

In the 1700s European thinkers argued that people should seek knowledge and freedom through using reason. This movement, known as the Enlightenment,

▶ This theater in the royal palace at Drottningholm opened in 1766. During the Enlightenment of the 1700s, the Swedish royal family was an enthusiastic supporter of the arts.

included Swedes such as the botanist Linnaeus and the physicist Anders Celsius. King Gustav III encouraged a golden age of the arts. Gustav III took back power from the Riksdag, but he made many enemies. He was murdered at a ball in 1792.

## A French King

In 1805 King Gustav IV joined an alliance with other European countries against France, then led by Napoleon Bonaparte. In 1809 Napoleon's Russian allies captured most of Finland, which had been part of Sweden since the 13th century. After the defeat, King Gustav IV was forced to give up his throne.

The new king, Charles XIII, had no children. The Swedish parliament elected the French soldier Jean-Baptiste Bernadotte as crown prince. He led Swedish troops as Sweden and its allies defeated Napoleon in

▲ A re-creation of a Viking longship floats in the harbor in front of the National Museum in Stockholm. The museum contains Swedish art from the last three centuries.

# JEAN-BAPTISTE BERNADOTTE

Jean-Baptiste Bernadotte was a lieutenant in the French army who served the French general and ruler Napoleon Bonaparte. In 1810 the Swedish Riksdag, or parliament, elected Bernadotte crown prince of Sweden. They hoped that he would restore Sweden to its glorious military past. King Charles XIII of Sweden, who had no children, adopted Bernadotte as his son. Bernadotte was regent during King Charles's last years. Then he became king himself in 1818. He took the name King Charles XIV of Sweden.

1813. As part of the peace settlement, Norway passed to Swedish control. The two countries were united until 1905. Bernadotte became King Charles XIV in 1818.

## Centuries of Change

Sweden's population grew rapidly in the 1800s, but there was not enough work. Thousands of emigrants left Sweden to find a new life. Between the 1850s and 1930s, 1.3 million Swedes settled in the United States.

Meanwhile, Sweden's economy improved. Railroads and canals made communication better. Sawmills and wood-pulping factories were the basis of Swedish industry.

▼ Swedes crowd the dockside in Göteborg in 1905 to say farewell to emigrants sailing for the United States.

In 1842 the Riksdag introduced free elementary schools. As Swedes became better educated, they joined political movements, workers' associations, and labor unions. In 1921 a long campaign won all Swedish adults the right to vote in parliamentary elections.

## The Swedish Model

In the 1900s industry developed fast. Many people moved to Stockholm, Malmö, Göteborg, and other cities to work. In 1936 Swedish politicians began to develop the welfare state. The government paid money to people who had no jobs or who were sick.

Sweden became famous for combining successful industry with good conditions for workers, thanks to strong labor unions and the welfare state. The combination is called "the Swedish model."

Today Sweden, like many countries, faces new challenges. Some Swedes want a more dynamic economy, but many Swedes still support the Swedish model. They believe that its basic intention to avoid severe inequalities is commonsensical. They see it as an important part of being Swedish.

## "COUNT US OUT!"

Sweden has officially been a neutral country since the mid-1800s, so it does not take sides in peace or war. The policy has brought decades of peace, but it has also caused problems. In World War I, Sweden traded with both sides until Britain and the United States imposed a trade ban, causing food shortages in Sweden. In World War II, Sweden sold valuable petroleum products to Nazi Germany. Today Sweden's army takes part in international peacekeeping operations.

▲ This Swedish solider served in a NATO peacekeeping force in Bosnia in 1996.

# Light
## *in the*
# Darkness

**O**N DECEMBER 13 Swedish children celebrate the Festival of Lights or St. Lucia's Day. A girl called the Light Queen puts on a crown of candles and a white robe. She leads a procession of girls carrying candles and boys wearing pointed hats topped with golden stars. They all sing carols in praise of St. Lucia. The Light Queen hands out gingersnaps and drinks. She represents the sun, which will return when winter turns to spring.

Swedish people enjoy celebrating the changing seasons. When spring arrives, they light bonfires to mark Walpurgis Night. In midsummer, they dance around maypoles with flowers in their hair. They enjoy an outdoor feast of herring, sour cream, and potatoes, along with fresh strawberries and cream.

◀ **The young woman chosen as the Light Queen arrives at a museum in Stockholm on St. Lucia's Day in 2005. Schools, workplaces, and towns all have their own light queens.**

## At a Glance

# PLENTY OF SPACE

Only around 9 million people live in Sweden, making it one of the least populated countries in Europe. Most people used to live in the country, but today 85 percent live in cities. Southern Sweden is home to large cities like Stockholm, Malmö, and Göteborg. Farther north, cities and towns are few and far between.

The population is growing. It will rise by about 20 percent by 2050, because of immigration and because Swedes are having more children. People are also living longer. By 2050, nearly a quarter of Swedes will be age 65 or older.

| 1950 / 7.0 million | 1970 / 8.0 million |
|---|---|
| 66% urban / 34% rural | 81% urban / 19% rural |

| 1990 / 8.6 million | 2005 / 9.0 million |
|---|---|
| 83% urban / 17% rural | 83% urban / 17% rural |

# Common Swedish Phrases

Here are a few words and phrases you might use in Sweden. Give them a try:

| | |
|---|---|
| Hello | Hej (hay) |
| Good-bye | Hej då/adjö (Hay-daw/ ad-JUH) |
| Please | Tack/Varsågod (tack/vahr- shawg-OOD) |
| Thank you | Tack (tack) |
| Pleased to meet you | Trevligt att träffas (trayv- litt att TREF-fas) |
| How are you? | Hur mår du? (Hewr mawr dew) |
| Well, thank you | Mycket bra, tack (MEW-keb brab, tack) |
| Excuse me | Ursäkta (Ewer-shekta) |
| I'm sorry | Förlåt (furr-LAWT) |

▼ **This cottage stands in a park at the southern end of the island of Gotland. One in four families living in Sweden's cities has another home in the countryside for weekends and vacations.**

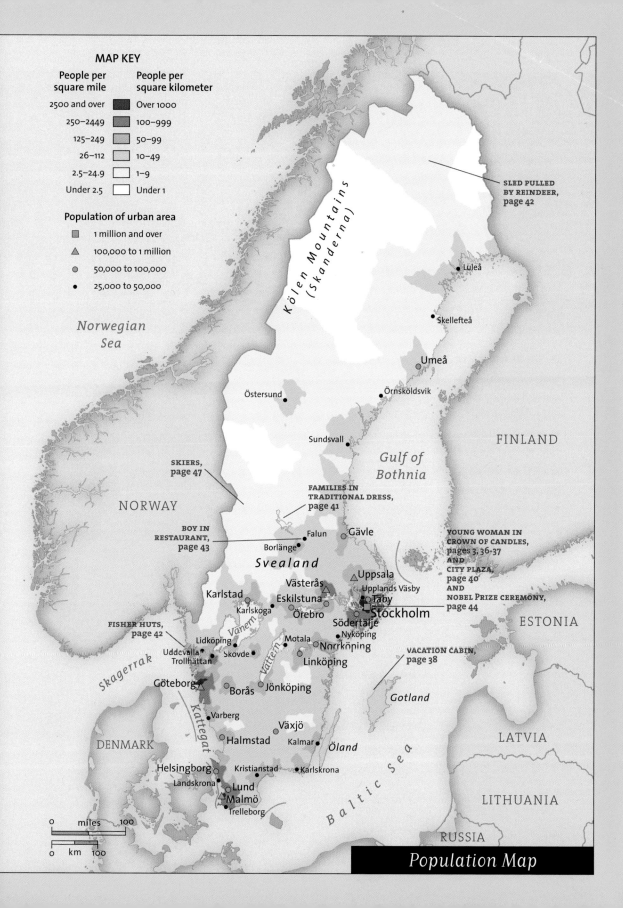

## MAP KEY

**People per square mile**    **People per square kilometer**

| | |
|---|---|
| 2500 and over | Over 1000 |
| 250–2449 | 100–999 |
| 125–249 | 50–99 |
| 26–112 | 10–49 |
| 2.5–24.9 | 1–9 |
| Under 2.5 | Under 1 |

**Population of urban area**

- ☐ 1 million and over
- △ 100,000 to 1 million
- ● 50,000 to 100,000
- • 25,000 to 50,000

SLED PULLED
BY REINDEER,
page 42

*Norwegian
Sea*

Luleå

Skellefteå

Umeå

Kölen Mountains
(Skanderna)

Östersund

Örnsköldsvik

Sundsvall

*Gulf of
Bothnia*

FINLAND

SKIERS,
page 47

FAMILIES IN
TRADITIONAL DRESS,
page 41

NORWAY

BOY IN
RESTAURANT,
page 43

Falun

Gävle

Borlänge

YOUNG WOMAN IN
CROWN OF CANDLES,
pages 3, 36-37
AND
CITY PLAZA,
page 40
AND
NOBEL PRIZE CEREMONY,
page 44

*Svealand*

Uppsala

Västerås

Uppland Väsby

Karlstad

Eskilstuna

Täby

Karlskoga

Örebro

Stockholm

FISHER HUTS,
page 42

Södertälje

Nyköping

*Vänern*

Lidköping

Motala

Norrköping

ESTONIA

Uddevalla
Trollhättan

Skövde

Linköping

*Vättern*

VACATION CABIN,
page 38

Göteborg

Borås

Jönköping

*Gotland*

Varberg

LATVIA

*Skagerrak*

*Kattegat*

Växjö

DENMARK

Halmstad

Kalmar

*Öland*

Helsingborg

Kristianstad

Karlskrona

*Baltic
Sea*

LITHUANIA

Landskrona

Lund

Malmö

Trelleborg

RUSSIA

| miles | |
|---|---|
| 0 | 100 |
| km | |
| 0 | 100 |

**Population Map**

▲ Sergels Torg is in the heart of Stockholm. Its main landmark is the glass obelisk, a tall sculpture erected in 1974. Much of the public space is in a sunken plaza beneath the road and fountains.

# Town and Country

In Swedish towns and cities, about half the people live in apartments. The tenants share washing machines and dryers in the basement. Outside, there are gardens and play areas for children. Most apartment buildings have an area for storing bicycles. On Saturdays in summer, families often drive to the country for a day out or to stay in a cottage. Almost half of all Swedes stay in a country or seaside cottage every year.

# Family and Festivals

Families are important in Sweden, particularly at the time of major festivals such as Midsummer, Easter, and Christmas. People invite family and friends to big parties and to eat traditional dishes. At midsummer they always try to eat outdoors, even if there are clouds in the sky. Nights are extremely short at midsummer, and people gather to watch the sun set and rise again

a few hours later. Young people sometimes pick nine different wild flowers and place them under their pillow when they go to bed. According to tradition, they will see their future husband or wife in their dreams.

On Maundy Thursday, before Easter Sunday, children dress up as witches and hand out Easter cards to friends and neighbors. In return they receive sweets or small gifts of money. On Easter Sunday, people eat decorated hard-boiled eggs.

On Christmas Eve Swedish families share a traditional meal of ham, *lutfisk* (a type of fish), and rice pudding. They dip bread in the broth left over from boiling the ham, a tradition called *dopp i grytan* (dope-ee gree-tahn), "dipping in the kettle."

Then children are ready for a visit from the *tomte*, their equivalent of Santa Claus. The tomte is a kind of gnome that people used to say lived under the floor of the barn and looked after cows and pigs on the farm.

# NATIONAL HOLIDAYS

**M**ost of Sweden's national holidays mark Christian festivals such as Christmas, Epiphany, and Ascension Day. Others, such as Midsummer Day, celebrate the passage of the seasons. Since the 1950s, Midsummer Day has officially been celebrated on the weekend nearest to June 24, but in some areas people always celebrate on the traditional date of June 23. Sweden's National Day only became a public holiday in 2005. It is celebrated with parades in most towns.

| | |
|---|---|
| **JANUARY 1** | New Year's Day |
| **JANUARY 6** | Epiphany |
| **MARCH/APRIL** | Maundy Thursday/Good Friday/Easter Sunday |
| **MAY 1** | May Day |
| **MAY** | Pentecost/Ascension Day |
| **JUNE 6** | National Day of Sweden |
| **JUNE** | Midsummer Day |
| **OCTOBER 31** | All Saints' Day |
| **DECEMBER 25** | Christmas Day |

▼ Families wear traditional costumes to celebrate midsummer at an outdoor festival near Siljan Lake.

▲ Ports like Smögen, on the east coast, supply the fish that is such an important part of the Swedish diet.

In many families, a person dresses as the tomte and brings in a bag of presents. People often leave a bowlful of rice pudding out for him.

## Swedish Food

People in different parts of Sweden have local specialties, but people everywhere traditionally eat berries and fresh foods in summer and root vegetables and preserved foods in winter.

# THE SÁMI AND SANTA CLAUS

Our Christmas traditions about Santa Claus are based on the midwinter festival of the Sámi who live in Lapland, a region that includes northern Sweden and parts of Norway, Finland, and Russia. Traditionally the Sámi were reindeer herders, although most now work in towns and cities for the government and in businesses.

Most Sámi today are Christian, but in the past they followed a pagan religion. At midwinter, Sámi priests took magical journeys on flying reindeer. They visited the tents of their tribe and went down the chimney holes to hand out gifts. In the same way, we say, Santa travels on a sleigh pulled by flying reindeer and climbs down chimneys to leave gifts. Santa's red cloak and fur-lined hat are based on the clothes worn by Sámi reindeer hunters.

▲ Santa's sleigh may be based on the reindeer sleds used by the Sámi to cross snowy landscapes.

Fish has always been an important food in Sweden. It appears in the best-known Swedish meal, the smörgåsbord. This self-service table includes herring, *gravad lax* (spiced raw salmon in dill), potatoes, cold meats, salads, and perhaps *Janssons frestelse* ("Jansson's temptation"), a casserole of onions, potatoes, anchovies, and cream.

Whatever they eat, Swedes often drink coffee. People in Sweden drink more coffee than anyone else in the world. They have a special word, *fika*, which means to take a break for coffee. They often have a cookie or a sandwich with coffee.

## Mothers at Work

In parks and supermarkets all over Sweden, you can see fathers looking after babies and young children. Eight out of every ten Swedish women go out to work. When a couple has a baby, both parents get paid time off work to share childcare during the first year.

Above the age of one, children usually go to day-care centers or *dagis*. There are places for all children up to age six. Parents leave home early to drop the children off at the dagis. Often they go by bicycle, with the children riding in seats on the back.

The Swedish government tries to make it easy for parents to combine work and family life. Sweden's

▲ A young Swede waits for the start of a Christmas smörgåsbord in Dalarna. The name of the feast comes from the Swedish word for "bread and butter table."

birth rate is one of the highest in Europe. People in Sweden always show respect toward children. There is a law against threatening or hitting children.

## Growing Up

Children start school at age six or seven. They have plenty of opportunities to play sports and to learn musical instruments. There are classes and practice sessions before and after school. There are only two semesters. They are divided by a Christmas holiday that lasts from mid-December to early January.

▲ The popularity of coffee has been encouraged by cafe chains that target young Swedes by providing a relaxing environment to hang out in.

At age 16, young people can choose whether to carry on studying or to learn skills useful for work. Nine out of ten Swedish children continue on from

## THE ULTIMATE AWARD

The 19th-century Swedish chemist Alfred Nobel invented dynamite and made a fortune, which he left in his will to pay for five prizes. The Nobel prizes have been given every year since 1901 for physics, chemistry, medicine, literature, and peacemaking. In 1968 a sixth prize was added, for economic sciences. Five prizes are decided in Sweden, but the winner of the peace prize is chosen by the Norwegian parliament. All six prizes are handed out in Stockholm's Konserthuset (concert hall) on December 10—the day Nobel died.

▲ The Swedish royal family (right) at the ceremony to award Nobel prizes.

compulsory school to upper secondary school, or *gymnasieskola,* until they are 19. Then they often go to college or university.

## Films, Books, and Music

Sweden is famous around the world for its moviemakers and stars. Two of the greatest movie stars of the 20th century, Greta Garbo and Ingrid Bergman, were Swedish. Director Ingmar Bergman made a series of famous films including *Wild Strawberries* and *The Seventh Seal* from the 1950s to the 1980s.

The country has also produced many well-known writers. In the late 19th and early 20th centuries August Strindberg wrote novels and plays that were acclaimed around the world. Beginning in the 1940s, Astrid Lindgren wrote children's books that were read by children in many countries. Her most famous character is a young girl called Pippi Longstocking.

## DAYS OF THE WEEK

In English, four of the days of the week are named after Norse gods once worshipped in Sweden. Tuesday was named for Tiu or Tyr, a war and sky god, and Wednesday for Woden or Odin, chief of the gods. Thursday was named after Thor, Odin's son and the god of thunder. Friday was named for Freyr, a fertility god linked to agriculture and the weather. Around a thousand years ago, people in Sweden worshipped images of Odin, Freyr, and Thor in a temple near Uppsala. Every nine years, they sacrificed men, horses, and dogs to the gods at the temple.

▼ Ingrid Bergman's most famous role was in *Casablanca* (1942) with Humphrey Bogart.

▶ Pippi Longstocking was created by Astrid Lindgren (right) as an unusual children's character. She is strong and rich, and likes to make adults who take themselves too seriously look foolish.

Many Swedes like folk music. At summer festivals, fiddlers play waltzes and polkas for dancing. The Swedes have even developed their own form of country music called *dansband musik*.

Sweden is famous for its pop music. The Swedish group ABBA was one of the best-selling bands of the 1970s and early 1980s. Other famous Swedish bands include Roxette, Ace of Base, the Cardigans, and Peter Björn and John.

# THANK THEM FOR THE MUSIC!

ABBA has sold more than 500 million records worldwide. The group's name was formed from the initials of the first names of its stars: Agnetha Fältskog, Benny Andersson, Björn Ulvaeus, and Anni-Frid Lyngstad. They first became an international hit in 1974, when their song "Waterloo" won the Eurovision Song Contest (a TV pop-music competition with entries from all over Europe). Their records topped the charts from the mid-1970s into the early 1980s. The band has not sung together since 1982 but their songs are still very familiar. The songs regularly appear in movies. *Mamma Mia!*, a musical show built around ABBA's songs, has been a smash hit around the world and was made into a movie. One of their last hits, in 1983, was the song "Thank You for the Music!"

▲ ABBA were so famous for their stage clothes that a museum of their costumes is due to open in Stockholm in 2009.

# Swedish Sports

Swedish people love hiking, swimming, cycling, horseback riding, canoeing, and sailing in summer. In winter they enjoy skiing and ice-skating. Babies are pulled along over the snow in buggies mounted on skis and children learn to ski when they've only just learned to walk. Swedes also like fishing, even in midwinter, when they fish through holes in the ice of frozen lakes.

Swedes also like ice hockey and soccer. The success of Swedish tennis star Björn Borg in the 1970s and early 1980s made tennis a major sport in Sweden. Children and young people play regularly and compete in tournaments.

▲ Skiers set out at the start of Vasaloppet, the world's biggest and longest cross-country ski race. On the first Sunday of every March, about 15,000 skiers tackle the 55-mile (90-km) course.

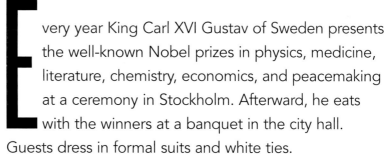

# King and Country

**E**very year King Carl XVI Gustav of Sweden presents the well-known Nobel prizes in physics, medicine, literature, chemistry, economics, and peacemaking at a ceremony in Stockholm. Afterward, he eats with the winners at a banquet in the city hall. Guests dress in formal suits and white ties.

The king of Sweden does not have any real power. His duties are ceremonial. He opens the yearly session of the Riksdag, or parliament, which governs the country. He also takes charge of the special council that meets when the government changes after an election. With his wife, Queen Silvia, King Carl XVI represents Sweden on visits to other countries and receives monarchs or heads of government when they visit Sweden.

◀ The ceremony of the changing of the guard at the Royal Palace in Stockholm is an echo of the days when the Swedish monarch had far more power than today.

# GETTING REPRESENTED

**M**any people get involved in politics in Sweden. There is a tradition of Swedes joining popular movements, or *folkrörelser*. A popular movement promoting temperance (attempts to limit or ban the sale of alcoholic drinks) was successful in the 1800s. In the 1900s, popular movements supported equality for women and labor unions. Anyone can set up a political party. All parties are funded by the government, which pays them a total of about $40 million a year. People are not allowed to donate money to political parties. Voting is by proportional representation, so each party has a number of members in the Riksdag based on its share of the vote. The parties are often closely balanced after an election, so they usually make deals to work together in a coalition government.

▲ From the Riksdaghuset, or parliament, arches lead to the streets of Stockholm.

## Trading Partners

**S**weden's most important trading partners are members of the European Union. It exports motor vehicles, paper products, wood, and chemicals. It imports machinery, petroleum products, raw materials for industry, and food.

| Country | Percentage of exports |
|---|---|
| European Union | 59.3 |
| United States | 9.3 |
| Norway | 9.1 |
| China | 1.9 |
| All others combined | 20.4 |

| Country | Percentage of imports |
|---|---|
| European Union | 70.3 |
| Norway | 8.5 |
| Russian Federation | 3.4 |
| United States | 3.4 |
| All others combined | 14.4 |

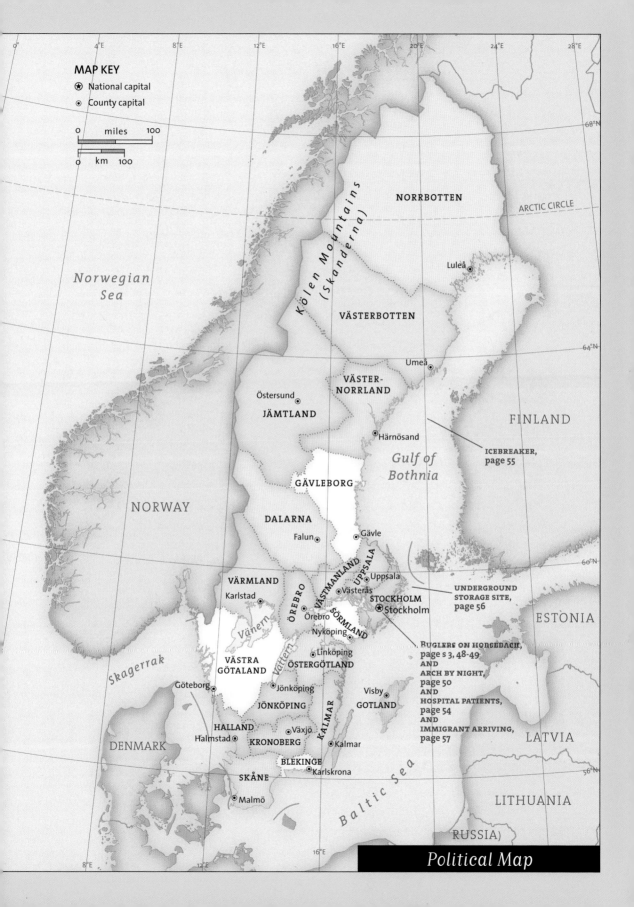

miles
0       100

km
0       100

Norwegian
Sea

Kölen Mountains
(Skanderna)

NORRBOTTEN

ARCTIC CIRCLE

68°N

Luleå

VÄSTERBOTTEN

64°N

Umeå

VÄSTER-
NORRLAND

FINLAND

Östersund

JÄMTLAND

Härnösand

Gulf of
Bothnia

ICEBREAKER,
page 55

GÄVLEBORG

NORWAY

DALARNA

Falun

Gävle

60°N

VÄSTMANLAND

UPPSALA

Uppsala

VÄRMLAND

ÖREBRO

Västerås

UNDERGROUND
STORAGE SITE,
page 56

Karlstad

STOCKHOLM
⊛ Stockholm

ESTONIA

Vänern

Örebro

SÖRMLAND

Nyköping

Vättern

BUGLERS ON HORSEBACK,
page s 3, 48-49
AND
ARCH BY NIGHT,
page 50
AND
HOSPITAL PATIENTS,
page 54
AND
IMMIGRANT ARRIVING,
page 57

Skagerrak

VÄSTRA
GÖTALAND

Linköping

ÖSTERGÖTLAND

Göteborg

Jönköping

Visby

GOTLAND

JÖNKÖPING

KALMAR

LATVIA

HALLAND

Växjö

Halmstad

KRONOBERG

Kalmar

DENMARK

BLEKINGE

Karlskrona

56°N

SKÅNE

Baltic Sea

LITHUANIA

Malmö

RUSSIA)

16°E

# Industrial Miracle

In 1900, Sweden was one of the poor countries of Europe. It depended almost completely on farming. But the country has changed remarkably. Today, Sweden has a successful industrial economy and Swedish companies are famous around the world. They include car and truck makers Saab and Volvo, furniture seller IKEA, telecommunications company Ericsson, and Electrolux, which makes refrigerators, washing machines, and other domestic appliances.

In the 1980s and early 1990s Swedish companies were so successful that they bought their rivals from

## HOW THE GOVERNMENT WORKS

Sweden is a constitutional monarchy. The king or queen is head of state, but the country is run by an elected government. The government is formed by members of the Riksdag, the Swedish parliament. There are 349 members in the Riksdag, who are elected by all Swedes over 18 years of age to serve for 4 years. The Swedish parliament only has one chamber. After an election, the members of the new parliament vote for a prime minister. The prime minister appoints the members of the cabinet. Each cabinet minister has particular responsibilities, such as for the economy, public health, or education. The prime minister and members of the cabinet appoint judges to the Supreme Court or Högsta Domstolen. The judiciary (justice system) is independent of the rest of government.

| GOVERNMENT | | |
|---|---|---|
| EXECUTIVE | LEGISLATIVE | JUDICIARY |
| PRIME MINISTER | RIKSDAG | HÖGSTA DOMSTOLEN |
| CABINET | | COURTS OF APPEAL, OR HOVRÄTTER |

# YOU CAN KEEP YOUR EURO

Sweden joined the European Union in 1995, but on September 14, 2003, Swedish voters rejected adopting the euro, the single European currency. People felt very strongly about the issue. About 8 out of 10 Swedes voted, with 56.1 percent against the euro and 41.8 percent in favor. Swedish business leaders and main political parties were in favor of the euro. Those who wanted to keep the krona thought that joining the euro might lead to losing Sweden's identity within Europe and might harm its economy.

▲ Campaigners against the euro celebrate the result of the vote in 2003.

other countries. IKEA took over British company Habitat in 1992, for example. Swedes were proud of this success. More recently, however, some Swedish companies have been sold to foreign firms. In 1999 Volvo sold its car-making business to the U.S. company Ford. Such sales worried some Swedes.

The sales were partly the result of economic difficulties in the first half of the 1990s. Many people lost their jobs. Welfare was expensive. In the mid-1990s, the government cut spending and tried to make the cost of Swedish goods lower. Since then the economy has recovered. Sweden is doing well again, especially in telecommunications, information technology (IT), and biotechnology.

▼ Shoppers visit an **IKEA** store in Shanghai, China. The furniture company leads the way in selling modern Swedish designs.

# THE WELFARE STATE

**M**ost Swedes are proud of how their government supports people in need. When a person is sick, he or she has to pay for medical care only up to a set limit. After that, all the costs are met by the government. Workers are paid 80 percent of their wages if they have to miss work because they are sick or have to look after sick children. Housing allowances help the elderly and the poor afford homes. People who have no job get benefits from their union or the government. Parents are entitled to 480 days of paid leave from work in the first eight years of their child's life. Either parent can take the leave, or they can share it between them. Elderly people, widows, and orphans are paid pensions.

▲ Hospital patients in Sweden sit in bright light to combat seasonal affective disorder—depression caused by darkness.

## At Work in Sweden

Swedish companies usually treat their employees well. Managers and workers are encouraged to work together. They share team-building exercises. Even top executives often wear casual clothes and have simple offices. They answer the telephone themselves rather than having a receptionist. The Swedish style of management is admired around the world.

There are very few strikes in Sweden. The government, workers, and industry leaders work closely to solve problems. Labor unions are very important to this system.

## Protecting the Environment

Most Swedish people love nature. Many Swedes try hard to make changes in industry and people's lifestyles that help protect the environment.

Swedish industry has invested a lot of money in reducing emissions that harm the environment. Companies have set up programs that protect nature. In Swedish homes, people recycle a lot of what they use. Most people separate their trash into food waste, paper, tin, and glass, which are all collected separately.

## Nuclear Energy

In the 1970s, the price of oil rose sharply around the world. Sweden decided to import less oil. Since then, most of its electricity has been produced by water power and nuclear power.

In March 1979, there was an accident at the Three Mile Island Nuclear Generating Station, a facility in Pennsylvania. This started a debate around the world about the safety of nuclear power plants. In 1980 the Swedes agreed in a national vote to phase out nuclear power by 2010. They became even more determined to do this after another nuclear

▲ Wood products make up 15 percent of Sweden's exports.

▼ An icebreaker leads a cargo ship through the frozen Gulf of Bothnia.

# INDUSTRY

**S**weden generates most of its electricity from hydroelectric plants. The country imports coal for purifying iron. The largest iron ore mines are in the north. The ore is brought south by train to steel mills near the main factories. The country's lumber mills are on the coast.

MAP KEY
- ⚙ Manufacturing center
- 🏭 Steel manufacturing

**Major Mines**
Fe  Iron ore

Norwegian Sea

Gulf of Bothnia

Fe

Steel
Västerås
Stockholm
Linköping
Göteborg

0    mi    200
0  km  200

Malmö

Baltic Sea

▼ Sweden's radioactive waste is buried deep beneath the Baltic Sea.

accident. In April 1986, explosions at the Chernobyl nuclear power plant in Ukraine spread radioactive material over many countries, including Sweden.

Sweden did not shut down all its nuclear power plants, however. The government closed two plants in 1999 and 2005, but in 2008 Sweden still had ten working nuclear power plants. Swedes still debate whether they should be closed, but there is no easy solution. The ten plants produce about half the country's electricity.

## Coping with Unemployment

In the 1970s and 1980s, most countries in Europe had poor economies and many people were out of work. However, Sweden was just the opposite. There were not enough people to take all the jobs. At this time immigrants came to Sweden to work. Many of the new arrivals were refugees from Chile, Palestine, Somalia, Iraq, and Iran, who were forced to move because of violence at home.

Sweden tried to give newcomers the same opportunities that Swedes enjoyed. However, when the country's economy began to fail in the 1990s, this became a big challenge. Many people, including new immigrants found it difficult to find work. By the mid-1990s, one person in ten in Sweden was without a job.

## A New Approach?

Some people began to call for a new approach. In September 2006 the Alliance for Sweden, a coalition or group of political parties led by the Conservative Party, took power from the Social Democrats who had dominated the government for nearly 70 years. Conservative Party leader Fredrik Reinfeldt became prime minister. The new government set out to boost the number of jobs and cut welfare benefits.

The Alliance for Sweden still supports the Swedish system of combining competitive industry with a strong welfare system, however. People around the world admire the Swedish system. Its success depends on the character of the Swedes. They are happy to use their common sense and to make compromises. Swedish people are proud of the system. They see themselves as setting an example that other countries could follow.

# SCANDAL AT SKANDIA

In 2003, Swedes were shocked by a scandal at the Swedish insurance company Skandia. Senior executives were accused of paying themselves large bonuses and using company money to renovate their own private apartments in Stockholm. Swedes were used to placing great trust in their business leaders, so the affair damaged public confidence in the economy. The Skandia chief executive Lars-Eric Petersson was imprisoned for fraud in May 2006, but later all charges against him were dismissed. Meanwhile, Skandia was taken over by a financial company based in South Africa and Britain.

▼ A health worker talks to a Kurdish woman from northern Iraq as she arrives to start a new life in Sweden in 2006.

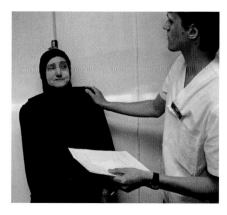

# Add a Little Extra to Your Country Report!

I f you are assigned to write a report about Sweden, you'll want to include basic information about the country, of course. The Fast Facts chart on page 8 will give you a good start. The rest of the book will give you the details you need to create a full and up-to-date paper or PowerPoint presentation. But what can you do to make your report more fun than anyone else's? If you use your imagination and dig a bit deeper into some of the topics introduced in this book, you're sure to come up with information that will make your report unique!

## >Flag

Perhaps you could explain the history of Sweden's flag, and the meanings of its colors. Go to **www.crwflags.com/fotw/flags** for more information.

## >National Anthem

How about downloading Sweden's national anthem and playing it for your class? At **www.nationalanthems.info** you'll find what you need, including the words to the anthem, plus sheet music for it. Simply pick "S" and then "Sweden" from the list on the left-hand side of the screen, and you're on your way.

## >Time Difference

If you want to understand the time difference between Sweden and where you are, this Web site can help: **www.worldtimeserver.com**. Select "Current Times" at the top of the page, then pick Sweden from the list at the right. If you called someone in Sweden right now, would you wake them up?

## >*Currency*

Another Web site will convert your money into krona, the currency used in Sweden. You'll want to know how much money to bring if you're ever lucky enough to travel to Sweden: **www.xe.com/ucc**.

## >*Weather*

Why not check the current weather in Sweden? It's easy—go to

**www.weather.com** to find out if it's sunny or cloudy, warm or cold in Sweden right now! Pick "World" from the headings at the top of the page. Then search for a city in Sweden, such as Stockholm. Be sure to click on the tabs above today's weather report for a satellite weather map, a record of yesterday's weather, and forecasts for tomorrow, 10 days ahead, or a month ahead. Compare your weather to the weather in the Swedish city you chose. Is this a good season, weather-wise, for a person to travel to Sweden?

## >*Miscellaneous*

Still want more information? Simply go to National Geographic's World Atlas for Young Explorers at **http://www.nationalgeographic.com/ kids-world-atlas**. It will help you find maps, photos, music, games, and other features that you can use to jazz up your report.

# Glossary

**Artificial**  describing something that has been made by people to do the same things as a naturally occuring item.

**Cabinet**  a group of politicians who run a country. Each member of the cabinet is called a minister and is in charge of a particular part of the government.

**Ceremonial**  a duty or ritual that is performed as a symbol of a belief or a power but has no other useful purpose.

**Climate**  the average weather of a certain place at different times of year.

**Culture**  a collection of beliefs, traditions, and styles that belongs to people living in a certain part of the world.

**Democracy**  a country that is ruled by a government chosen by all its people through elections.

**Economy**  the system by which a country creates wealth through making and trading products.

**Endangered**  an animal or plant that is at risk of dying out.

**Exported**  transported and sold outside the country of origin.

**Glacier**  a body of ice formed over thousands of years, mainly by layers of snow, that slowly flows on land.

**Hostel**  an inexpensive hotel where the customers—often young people—sleep in large communal rooms.

**Imported**  brought into the country from abroad.

**Livestock**  farm animals.

**Longship**  a seagoing Viking ship powered by oars and a square sail and steered with a large board on the right side.

**Monarchy**  a system of government that is headed by a king or queen.

**Peninsula**  a narrow piece of land that is surrounded by water on three sides. The word means "almost island" in Latin.

**Root vegetable**  a vegetable made up mainly of the root of a plant. Common root vegetables are potatoes, carrots, and rutabagas.

**Scandinavia**  a region of northern Europe that is made up of peninsulas formed by Sweden, Norway, and Denmark. Finland and the Kola Peninsula of western Russia are sometimes included as part of the region, and Iceland is also added because it is populated by mainly Scandinavian people.

**Species**  a type of organism; animals or plants in the same species look similar and can only breed successfully among themselves.

**Strait**  a narrow strip of sea that runs between two pieces of land.

**Sulfur**  a substance that is found in many naturally occuring substances, such as rocks and wood. Sulfur-containing substances are generally bad smelling and are released as pollution by many factories.

**Union**  an agreement between regions or countries to join together as a single state.

**Welfare state**  a social-security system that provides money and housing for people who do not have jobs or are too ill to work.

# Bibliography

Alexander, Vimala. *Welcome to Sweden*. Milwaukee, WI: Gareth Stevens, 2002.

Gan, Delice, and Leslie Jermyn. *Sweden*. New York, NY: Benchmark Books, 2003.

Keeler, Stephen. *Sweden*. Chicago, IL: Raintree, 2005.

Porterfield, Jason. *Sweden: A Primary Source Cultural Guide*. New York, NY: Rosen Publishing Group, 2004.

http://www.sweden.se (an English-language Web site about the country)

http://www.sweden.gov.se/ (official government Web site)

# Further Information

## NATIONAL GEOGRAPHIC Articles

Quammen, David. "Carl Linnaeus: A Passion for Order." NATIONAL GEOGRAPHIC (June 2007): 72-87.

## Web sites to explore

More fast facts about Sweden, from the CIA (Central Intelligence Agency): https://www.cia.gov/library/publications/the-world-factbook/geos/sw.html

Sweden has been ruled by kings and queens since the 12th century. The current king can trace his ancestry back to 1818. Find out more about the Swedish monarchy, meet the members of the country's royal family, and see where they live using their official Web site: http://www.royalcourt.se

Do you want to see what is happening in Sweden right now? This excellent Web site has links to many Webcams trained on the country. This one is looking at Sergels Torg in Stockholm: http://www.webbkameror.se/webbkameror/sergelstorg/index.php. Click on "webbkameror—start" to select another location.

Sweden has many festivals and celebrations throughout the year. Find out more about what happens on Midsummer Day and other special days at: http://www.sweden.se/templates/cs/CommonPage _ _ _ _11366.aspx

## See, hear

There are many ways to get a taste of life in Sweden, such as movies and music. You might be able to locate these:

*Radio Sweden*
This radio station broadcasts some programs in English. There are also podcasts to download from the Web site: http://www.sr.se/rs/english/index.htm

*The Seventh Seal (1957)*
Regarded by experts as one of the best movies ever made, this black-and-white drama by Swedish director Ingmar Bergman tells the story of a knight and his servant returning after years of war only to find their people dying from disease. When Death, or the Grim Reaper, comes to claim the pair, they challenge him to a game of chess to buy more time and find a way to defeat him. The imagery from this movie—such as the pale face and dark cloak of Death— is familiar even to people who have never seen the movie.

# Index

# Credits

## Picture Credits

Front Cover – Spine: Anders Sjomon/Shutterstock; Top: Pawel Kopczynsky/Reuters/Corbis; Low Far Left: Staffan Widstrand/Corbis; Low Left: Matthias Schrader/dpa/Corbis; Low Right: Kevin Schafer/Corbis; Low Far Right: Dan Holmberg/Corbis.

Interior – Corbis: 34 lo; Art Archive: 32up; Bibikow/JAI: 2-3, 24-25; Christophe Boisvieux: 26 up; Elio Ciol: 34 up; Jon Hicks: 50 lo; Francis Joseph/Sygma: 10 up; Pawel Kopczynsky/Reuters: 2 right; Massimo Listri: 32 lo; Pontius Lundahl/epa: 44 lo; Tim Page: 35 right; Ulf Palm/epa: 47 up; Frederic Pitchal/Sygma: 56 lo; Steve Raymer: 10 lo; Scott T. Smith: 20 lo; Paul Souders: 53 lo; Hubert Stadler: 41 lo; Hans Strand: 2 left, 6-7; Sunset Boulevard: 45 lo; Henrick Trygg: 13 right; : Staffan Widstrand: 16-17; Adam Woolfitt: 42 up; Bob Zaunders: 43 right;  Getty Images: Pressens Bild/AFP: 46 left; Jan Collsioo/AFP: 53 up; Peter Grant: 14 lo; Ollie Lindberg/AFP: 46 lo; Sven Nackstrand/ AFP: 3 left, 36-37; Kevin Palsson/AFP: 15 right; Tomasz Tomaszewski/NGIC: 57 lo; Konrad Wothe: 55 up; NGIC: Sisse Brimberg & Cotton Coulson/Keenpress: 11 lo; 12 up, 28 lo, 31 lo, 44 up, 55 lo; Dean Conger: 30 up; Cotton Coulson: 23 lo; Gordon Graham: 29 up; Louis S. Glanzman: 29 lo; Anne Keiser: 3 right, 48-49; Mattias Klum 20 up, 22 up, 22 lo, 23 up; Albert Moldvay: 30 lo; Panoramic Stock Images: 12 lo; 14 up, 42 up; Richard Norrtiz: 5 up, 33 up, 40 up; Norbert Rosing: 18 lo, 21; Tomasz Tomaszewski: 46 up, 54 up: Priit Vesilind: TP, 38 lo; Shutterstock: Mikael Damker: 59 up;

For information about special discounts for bulk purchases, contact National Geographic Special Sales: ngspecsales@ngs.org

For more information, please call 1-800-NGS-LINE (647-5463) or write to the following address:

NATIONAL GEOGRAPHIC SOCIETY
1145 17th Street N.W.
Washington, D.C. 20036-4688 U.S.A.

Visit us online at www.nationalgeographic.com/books

Library of Congress Cataloging-in-Publication Data available on request
ISBN: 978-1-4263-0389-0

Printed in the United States of America

Series design by Jim Hiscott.
The body text is set in Avenir; Knockout.
The display text is set in Matrix Script.

Front Cover—Top: Santas compete at the annual Wintergames at Gallivare; Low Far Left: Bull moose shedding its antlers; Low Left: IKEA employee reads catalog on IKEA chairs; Low Right: Viking longship, Stockholm; Low Far Right: Fishers' huts at Smögen

Page 1—Boat rental dock, Skansen Park, Stockholm; Icon image on spine, Contents page, and throughout: Herring

## Produced through the worldwide resources of the National Geographic Society

John M. Fahey, Jr., *President and Chief Executive Officer*; Gilbert M. Grosvenor, *Chairman of the Board*; Tim T. Kelly, *President, Global Media Group*; John Q. Griffin, *President, Publishing*; Nina D. Hoffman, *Executive Vice President, President of Book Publishing Group*

## National Geographic Staff for this Book

Nancy Laties Feresten, *Vice President, Editor-in-Chief of Children's Books*
Bea Jackson, *Director of Design and Illustration*
Jim Hiscott, *Art Director*
Virginia Koeth, *Project Editor*
Lori Epstein, *Illustrations Editor*
Stacy Gold, Nadia Hughes, *Illustrations Research Editors*
R. Gary Colbert, *Production Director*
Lewis R. Bassford, *Production Manager*
Nicole Elliott, *Manufacturing Manager*
Mapping Specialists, Ltd., *Maps*

## Brown Reference Group plc. Staff for this Book

*Volume Editor: Tom Jackson*
*Designer: Dave Allen*
*Picture Manager: Sophie Mortimer*
*Maps: Martin Darlison*
*Artwork: Darren Awuah*
*Index: Kay Ollerenshaw*
*Senior Managing Editor: Tim Cooke*
*Children's Publisher: Anne O'Daly*
*Editorial Director: Lindsey Lowe*

## About the Author

CHARLES PHILLIPS has written more than 25 books, mainly about history, archaeology, and myth. He lives in London with his young family. He has also written *Countries of the World: Japan* for National Geographic.

## About the Consultants

SUSAN C. BRANTLY is a professor of Scandinavian literature at the University of Wisconsin in Madison. Her research focuses on Swedish literature with a special emphasis on contemporary historical fiction. She has written books on the authors Laura Marholm (1992) and Isak Dinesen (2002). She lived in Sweden for over three years and has made many research visits there.

ERIC CLARK is a professor of human geography at Lund University, Sweden. His research focuses on urban social geography, the political economy of space and the historical political ecology of island societies. Professor Clark is Fellow of the Royal Society of Letters at Lund and editor of *Geografiska Annaler Series B: Human Geography*. His recent publications include book chapters in *Reanimating Places: A Geography of Rhythms* (2004), *Gentrification in a Global Context: The New Urban Colonialism* (2005) and *A World of Islands: An Island Studies Reader* (2007).

# Time Line of
# Swedish History

## B.C.

**ca 1600** The inhabitants of Scandinavia learn to work bronze; they trade with central and southern Europe to get the tin and copper to make the metal.

**ca 500** Scandinavian smiths begin to make objects out of iron, which is easily found in Sweden.

## A.D.

**ca 100** Goths migrate from Scandinavia to the region north of the Black Sea and trade with the Roman empire.

**ca 500** The Vendel culture grows with the fall of the Roman empire. Their Norse myths featuring warrior gods spread through Sweden.

**793** Viking seafarers raid the British monastery of Lindisfarne. The raid marks the beginning of three centuries of Viking attacks in Europe.

## 1000

**1008** Olof Skötkonung declares himself king of Sweden.

**1255** Swede Birger Jarl founds Stockholm, a city of brick that reflects the influence of the Hanseatic League, a union of trading centers in northern Germany.

**1350** The Black Death, a form of plague, arrives in the ports of Scandinavia; it kills many thousands of people.

**1397** Queen Margaret of Sweden establishes the Kalmar Union by making arrangements for her nephew, Erik of Pomerania, to be the ruler of Denmark, Sweden, and Norway.

## 1400

**1430s** The Swedish Parliament is founded.

**1477** Uppsala University is founded to train Swedish men for a life in the clergy.

## 1500

**1520** In the "Stockholm Bloodbath," Christian II of Denmark kills 82 Swedish nobles and attempts to take control of Sweden.

**1523** Gustav Eriksson Vasa leads a rebellion that drives Christian II out of Sweden. He is crowned King Gustav I.

**1544** The Swedish crown becomes hereditary.

**1550** Gustav I establishes the port of Helsinki in modern-day Finland to increase trade that comes from Russia on its way to Northern Europe.

**1562** Sweden claims Riga, in current day Latvia, expanding its control over the Baltic region and its trade.

**1593** Uppsala University decrees Sweden to be a Lutheran country.

## 1600

**1630** Sweden joins the Thirty Years' War and wins control of the German territories of Pomerania, Wismar, Bremen, and Verden.

## 1700

**1700** The Great Northern War begins as a conflict between Russia and Sweden for control of the Baltic Sea and its trade.